To My Lady

And other

poems

by

Joseph Will Carney

To Anne

Introduction

I started many years ago mainly in
Ohio, Virginia and California. I have come
to appreciate my parents, friends, teachers,
colleagues, and my loves through this
experience. Now in retirement, since July
2007, and living in Bangkok, Thailand, The
Land of Smiles, I have seen the beauty of
Southeast Asia, the wonder of natural
places, the kindness from people's hearts,
the curiosity of "same same" and
"different", the longing for acceptance, the
magic of Temples, the purity of souls, and
the everlasting fortune to have chosen
Southeast Asia, or did it choose me?

This wondrous journey to self-publish has taken me to create my website, www.wix.com/jwillcarney/poppop, to host my blog, www.wix.com/jwillcarney/poppop/apps/blog, and activate jwillcarney@gmail.com.

I held three contests to have a book cover designed and was thrilled to have 10 designers and 83 designs. I could not have selected one design without my friends from Asia and America,
especially my former colleagues from Alexander Hamilton High School, LAUSD, CA.
My kindle book is alive as of today, March 17, 2002 with amazon.com. Yes, there is a book 2.

Contents

Shrugging at the bar
On plutonic elegance
Statues in Pershing Square
Wishes in time and space
On regained life
After the first kiss
Reaching beyond eternity
Greater than the sum
On respect
On concern
On appearance of sadness
On finding a clue
On deliverance of children
From a sailor son
Navy life after taps
One-oh-one
A watch on life and death

SANCTUARY OF THE SOUL

And I saw the birds fly
Way over the sky did soar.
My heart did cry when I did see
An arrow to her from my door.

Oh weep did I retrieve her soul
Before a cat did prey
To eat her flesh, to clean her bones,
Her feathers to scatter away.

Her heart was laid, an open wound.
My tears washed the stain.
My tears did flow upon her soul,
A death that life has slain.

All alone tonight I'l cry,
Oh bless this life I love.
And take me now to my abode
To heaven, to her up above.

VEIL OF HONOR

Your breath fills me with hope
And desire for you. Each breath hypnotized
My mind and released thoughts of you.

You are dear to me. Your heart fills
Me like the river of love fills the western
Lakes and reservoirs. Your heart tells
Me, implores me to stay, make no exodus.
Drink the cherry water of your breath.

Your heart returns like the final chord
Of thousands whispering
High notes of love. Thoughts of you fill
Me with sounds of bellowing horns,
Recapture days already gone, a royal love.
The harp salutes our love and plucks the
Finality of love. Your nearness causes
A sway of orchestras at crescendo, then
Diminuendo and grace.

An endless cascade of rushing strings
Send our love soaring on
The outskirts of worlds.

WE WENT ON

I remember a cold winter day,
Shortly after Christmas had passed
When I ran to say,
Stay.

My thoughts torment me at the near loss;
I sweat, stare, and pain.

They wanted us to toss love aside like
Unpaired shoes.

We went on.

The minister, the Holy Beast,
The angelic garb, their agent,
The narrator of
Our lives.

We went on.

To wrench us apart,
He aligned with them.

We went on.

WHEN THE SUN LEAVES THE UNIVERSE

Every thought is thought of you.
If I could be the core of all,
You would be the center too,
You would be the forest mall.

If I could soar through the night,
You would hold the day at the gate.
If I should fall when in my flight,
You would catch and save your mate.

You are mighty both strong and near,
As strong as rock and always hear
My call to you. You are here
Surrounding my thoughts so dear.

REALIZATION OF US

Let us prepare, we are not unique.
We are not the center
Of the Universe.

We are us, that's all.

But, being us is the most
Important ones we could ever be.

Others face life like we sought.
Their success is seen in them. They live and the
Earth still revolves. They talk
And sun still rises and sets.
They make fun and laughter with the world.

The rain falls and rainbows appear.
The sky is still once more.

Being us is no harder than being
Separate. We can exist in our world.
We are a part of this scheme of life
We fashioned yesterday.
Look back. We started and planned well.
No plans need be changed for health and wealth.

Our steps are unsure, but the way is
Safe, wide and straight.

Go on. Together we can face
Tomorrow. Apart we find only yesterday.

THE ART OF PAINTING

Picasso painted what he saw in the
Universe in one painting- a manifest
Truth. He created expressions in one
Swift stroke of a mighty brush. Three
Eyes peer down on us.

Not unusual though. Expressions change
Before the artist finishes his canvas,
So he chooses to paint yesterday and
Tomorrow as one day.

Manic depressions, sleepless nights,
Fevers and a period of blues for
Dress, blues for eyes, blues for hair,
Blues for the sun. Van Gogh's fever
In his yellow sun, yellow flowers, his
Yellow day, his sicknesses.

Painted the mind, they tried as it
Closed in on them as the nights and
Days passed into the brush, as the
Colors fused as the hues separated.

A state of color, a state of mind.

WILD WIND

Cry out wild wind of season.
Tell me the way to
Fly over the wind to her
Hideaway home.

Cry out wild wind of season
With a wind song of
Admiration. Life winds
On today to meet the
Jagged end of time.

Cry out wild wind of the season to
Me. Cry out old wild wind.
Your whirling voice pierces the
Center, the eye, the broad way
Of me with love. Behold, tidal waves
Push winds of gracious covering.

Cry out wild wind of season
And blanket my naked love.

A YEAR OF CANDLES

Each day is shorter when I am alone,
Whether I in the sun or under a dome.
If you would come, there would be no time.
Each day would pass without a chime.

You would be my heart, my soul, my cares.
I would live on strings, like puppet players.
Each day would come as day must come,
They would flow all into one.
Be here next year to hear me say
You make each day, my festive birthday.

WHY DO HEROES DIE

He had hopes of being a hero. He
Wanted to do what others thought.

He even talked of noble deeds,
Acts of courage, acts of valor. Wars
Record such deeds. (Most heroes are dead.)

He had his moment to act, but fled. No words
Were spoken of his hasty retreat.

I led his men beyond the hill, their tears
Filling the air to the bursting shrills of shells,
Men in battle stunned.

We ran and met the challenge. We did
His noble deeds, acts of strength, acts of valor.
When shall we die?

UPON A COWARD

He sipped of fame, but threw the cup
Down. He turned his back to the heights
Desired by men of the ages.

He spoke the words of deeds to do,
To men who followed strongly. Their
Deeds were done, a fearless lot,
To save the world from rot.

But a time comes nigh when all must do
The words one freely speaks.
But run did he away from the fight,
His deeds did go astray.

I stood and fought beside them,
Our tears rolling fast. A man did
Die this day. Their hearts were
Heavy with sorrow.

To the front I ran. A man may
Go the lesser way but deeds go
Straight ahead. Hear the words
Of men today. Tomorrow,
We follow their deeds.

UPON A STAR

Look for a star where my
Heart rides high over the sky.
Beware of the night. My love
Twinkles in the light for you.

Moon let your light shine in the night.
Make the day disappear. Bring
My love near. Moon, shine
Your beam on her face for me.

Stand and let me see your love
In the moon's light.

TO A RETIRING PROFESSOR

Though your life may pass, we'l remember until,
How days did pass, as we from the
Window sill, looked on the
Campus toward Grey Chapel.

Our mixtures boiled with
The odor of chemists and
Researchers, brains at work, waiting
For the final bell, to ring, ring, ring.

But on and on we strode to identify the ion
That precipitated when
The pH was reached.

We made smells of hints of fruits
All because we knew
That June would come soon,
Soon, soon, soon, soon.

To you, we owe,
Never to repay, those years,

These years, and tomorrow.

NATURE IS A SPLENDID TREASURE

Love is more to people than pleasing.
The richest treasure he beholds, his treasure,
Must be inspiration, recipient, and
Responder to the sweet bird of love.
We live for this love. It completes
Our tragic lives.

I gave to you a golden-red leaf which
Sang to me as I turned to climb the
Stairs to Orchesis. I saw rapturous delight
When your slender fingers caressed
Its tender stem. Your radiant glow
Vibrated your body into a rhythmic sway,
Like a graceful swan. My arm rose to bless
The night and that noble tree which stood
There, tall and mighty. It gave one of
Its own to me, a leaf filled with untold
Bliss, golden-green, red, golden-red
Bliss. All were tinted with hues of
Teasing yellow and heavenly
Moods of orange.

That night, my soul leaped and danced
Gleefully across the universe. My mind
Joined in the merry chase to the
Mountain top. I waltzed and collapsed

In total submission to the beat of
The drum. Then slowly, one, two,
Three, four, my chin winged its way
To the sky. I soared to the
Blushing stars, dedicated to the grace
Of life. Motion was christened. I
Slowly arose and swam around, darting here
And there, then stillness.

You wanted to talk that night,
But I declined. The rain beat down on
Us. The night ended.

THE FIRST STEP OF LOVE

None had ever appeared as bright as
The star, which shone that night, when we
First realized, that together
We were one.

We sat there, remembering how long
Before it all began. We said no that
Day in Chapel, this can never be,
Because —
Then suddenly we realized the immense pain
Of our lives and decided. The fondness of
Yesterday is still here, more inviting
Than yesterday and growing stronger as
The day sinks with the sun into her
Misty night. The rain on the Great
Porch of Austin drifted down on us.

So, hurriedly we began to entertain
From the vast experiences we never had.
I held your hand when none could see.
But, as we passed, and saw the lights in their
Windows, we parted and knew our togetherness
Was one of secret and newness.

As their door opened into the night,
We parted around a tree until they

Disappeared. But, I kissed you later,
I knew the stars would never tell
Our secret to those waiting ears
Sitting on your bed, hoping,
Waiting, thinking, and fearing what
We feared and dared to do.

When you told them, they knew that things
Would seem strange until they
Became accustomed to our life.

And now, apart we sit, wondering where
We should have become one forever,
Instead of thinking, waiting, and
Making life unreal for others. But we
Knew at Christmas they would say
No, so we went on without them and
Succeeded until-

Now we hope and wait until something
Happens so others will know that
Life will be loneliness.

A POEM FROM ANNE

Conformity, a prison of four sheik beige walls,
Geometric designs, is the trap of
Thinking, "it's all right".
We'l do it your way even
Though I know I am right."

Bitter, despairing loneliness in an
Environment of luxury. The
Bitterness of defeat of a dream-
The tragedy of no hope- The
Realization of a world of loneliness
Inhabited by people out to
Make a buck- The sacrifice of humanity
For the almighty dollar.

There is no absolute dream. There
Is no millennium. It is a fantasy of the
Poets, something you want to believe.
It is, in reality, a world of compromise.
The truth is learning to be satisfied
With the good enough, learning to accept
The stark reality of disappointment.

There is no God, no romantic love,
No truth. There is only the power
Symbol, the bawdy laughter, the
Drizzling rain.

Spring is not the season of
Humanity- winter is that season-
The season of death.

For God's sake insignificant dreamer,
Grow up! Learn to live with your
Jolly fellow man. Do you want to
Spend the eternity of your life
In the arms of an illusion? Do not
Search for the perfect; find that
Which you can bear easily- This is
The secret of living.

Life can be a merry picnic- But first
You have to learn the lesson. It is
Very clear- one word only- conform.

Forget the luxury of weeping.

TO MY LADY

Had it not been for the love we shared,
I would say My Lady was fickle.
Be not so shy as to close the
Door to love's light and me.

Reward yourself with exquisite satins
And silk. Adorn your head with
Rubies and pearls and venture
Out to pick flowers by the pond.

A sparkling sun overhead and the glorious
Grass under foot, My Lady make
Your song gleeful. And walk lightly.
Kiss the daisies with dainty toe.

Regain your composure. Sit awhile in
The crisp air and breathe a sigh
Of contentment. The birds will fill your
Empty thoughts for tomorrow.

You should toss a petal to the pond and pursue
A butterfly across the lawn. Take
A swing on the Austin Gate and
Lift your petticoat high.

A secluded bath in the running spring
Will add color to your lips.
Now sleep MY LADY in the evening
Sun and awaken to the evening fowl.

Arise, MY LADY, to foods on the
Long table I set before the
Fire. A drink of wine perhaps to
Color your cheeks with fire.

To bed and lo, the stars twinkle
Across the bed, and a moon ray
Filters to your head. The
Night songbird sings.

Dream, MY LADY, of yesterday and
Joys to come. Dream while
I dream of you. Peaceful dreams
Of purest thoughts and me.

Arise, MY LADY, arise to restored
Health, wealth and youth. Waste
Not time this glorious morning.
A sip of juice and your bonnet, MY LADY.

MY LADY has since not cared for the
Dreary room of poems of lost loves
And life thereafter. (She only laughs
Today and hastens sleep for tomorrow.)

Her day drags no longer, like the
Train of her black gown. Grieve
She did over the great loss of her
Love who said, "I DO".

A splendid choice you did make, MY
LADY, of family, of wealth. Of great
Stature was he, broad brow, glaring
Eyes and smile of love and thrill.

A clever man with fortune, money flowed
To him for you. Cherish you, he did.
Love and child he did give to you
To bear his name and fame.

But fate did conquer your womb and
Take the life from you before
A breath he could take to live. A
Dark curtain was thrown over you.

Before the mist had cleared away, a new
Love had encircled your bed and took
Your last night's warmth, a love
Never to rouse life in you again.

To mourn so soon another, MY LADY.
How did He expect you to
Continue with so heavy a stone
Upon your breast and neck?

How did He ever think a sweet life
Could endure without a
Pulsating force? Did He not
Unite the two as one?

(Why then did Thou so suddenly take
Her two lovers from her body
And bed and take them to the
Cold earth of death and decay?)

Forgive me. I only ask to comfort
MY LADY, when she openly flings
The door and retires alone to
The bed where joy did dwell.

Be sure, again MY LADY shall find
A heart, as pure as the
One you took for thy own room,
To guard the little one perhaps.

"MY LADY"! What joys radiate from
Your brow, and "MY LADY, MY LADY"?
What tragic day
Took your petticoat?

What tree tore your dress and threw
Dirt on your face? Where did
You gather wild flowers, and
Lose a shoe in the pond perhaps?

Sit MY LADY and I'l caress your
Bruises and tend you. To bathe
You, refresh you, perfume you,
For your day's rest "My Lady".

Returned you did to conformity, to
Do what they desire. But your
Heart lingers far beyond the
Austin gate with me upon a star.

Despair, bitter loneliness awaits MY
LADY, your sacrifices to a world
Of compromise. (I wish not to join.
I will linger among the poets.)

MY LADY, squeeze an illusion and
Taste of beauty and
A successful life. (Turn your
Hand from the almighty buck.)

Refrain from doing what she may
Suggest, making the beige
Hall ring with song. Open the
Window to the bright light of me.

May I suggest MY LADY,
Perhaps, joining you with
The love you deserve. Our fellow
Man would then join you in song.

I'l protect you with strong armor,
With rays of love, a broad arm to
Hold you, my heart to shield you.
My life will protect you always.

Pick up the flower MY LADY, near your
Hand it blooms. Gently raise it to
Your bosom. Its fragrance will soon
Soothe your troubled soul.

The season is for loving. The stagnant winter
Has washed away the stains of
Death. Eternity is blooming in the
Perfect light of love.

Simplicity with elegance MY LADY,
With one who travels the path
Of the living. Rest your arm on my
Shoulder, we start at dawn.

Weep MY LADY. I weep with
My eyes focused on love.
Forever together, never to
Part, until death, does decree.

UPON A BITTER EARTH

Bitter is the earth to me when it
Nourishes not my love. The
Land is ripe and rain falls.
The sun shines and the wind toils
Over the earth in its season.

Did I not pay homage to the Earth,
Prostrate my love to its bosom?
Did I not pray incessant, tearing
Prayers of gratitude to the Earth
Of summer, to the Earth of spring and
Earth of fall?

Did I not fall back in the eleventh month
Of the year and offer
Special thanks to induce Her to
Receive my seed of love eternal? Did
I not more abundantly consecrate
My Affection, my heart, my soul and my
Life for the maturity of this one seed?

Have I not since then returned to thank
Her and wait for the time
To send the sprouts of my love?
Loyal was I and shall remain to my love.

But loyal to you oh Bitter Earth, I can no longer
Be. For time, ceases to
Repeat like the seasons which die and
Return full of life giving. I must
Nourish that seed with water from a
Foreign heaven. The soil I will gather
Where neither feet nor oxen have trod.
The winds of a foreign breath will surround the
Seasons, seasons of hope, and magnanimity,
Truth, trust, and all their brothers, and
Send a breath and sigh to the new creation.

This new age will nourish and shelter the
Growth of that special seed, that new
Life-lasting, that love-eternal. To
Kneel no more to the old, but stand
With the new and be loved.

Bitter Earth, taste the sweetness of love.

SYMPHONY OF THE SIRE

My heart is as free as the dove
Soaring across the forest, for
My heart feels the symphony of life.

I stand here and listen to secrets
Whispering though the forest. I try
To absorb them before the
Orchestra ends.

"Love, no matter what the tone
Of the union can be killed", whispers
The hierarchy of the pines. The
Silver branch of everlasting shall unite
The two in everlasting life.

The roots quiver. The forest chatters in
Expectation of a new symphony born of
Wisdom. The theme is heard. Life is
Anchored in true love. The
Two are united from the first chord
To the splendid finale.

The leaves vibrate in concert to the
Pulsating Earth. The nakedness of the
Sire has been played.

The Sire has sung his aria. The branches,
With their extended knowledge, twist and
Reach for the tail of the wind. New
Light is given and must resonate through
The forest. The leaves, fluttering
Incessantly, harmonize their hues and
Attract the attention of the wind.

The chorus has begun. Union has been
Made. Time is yet old and wise. The
Trees reverberate with magnificent pitch.
Time is set. All play magnificently.
The Sire, filled with music
Of the forest, entreats the listener
With notes of love.

But the wind plays a sour note and blows,
With its horn throated force, the
Symphony out to sea. The waters gladly
Receive the message. Down into its
Innermost bowels, a lesson
Of the sage is lost.

All is rest. The forest exhausts its sway.
The wind respires. The waters no
Longer pitch and thunder. The forest is
Silent. Tears ripple to the Sire,
But no more does He listen and
Give wisdom.

A dove flies and rests on the
Uppermost branch only to flutter away
In fright. No welcome has the
Forest for purity this day. The Sire's
Words, seldom given, are lost.

Perhaps, when leaves have been tossed
About in ages of time, we shall hear the
Words of the Sire in his splendor. To
Recapture this fleeting moment,
We cannot.

A dove flies and rests with song
On the uppermost branch of the evergreen,
The heart of the forest.

ON DECIDING

Before taking that exceptional someone,
Decide.

Decide on the totality, which is
Readily seen, that can extend
To the last moment of time.

Examine the possibilities with him,
Decide on the limits of exhaustion,
The rate of temper, the capacity for
Love, the need for understanding.
Decide on all he can do.

Having decided on him, swim in the
Sea of wealth until your toes point
Toward the setting sun.

When the last second ticks, will
It ring the same ring as the first,
A ringing of the heart?

ON WATCHING A SMILE

Sitting, I saw a smile
Loom across his face. I was
Perplexed. What thoughts
Possessed him a moment ago
When he watched them parade, I asked?
To ask such a question is foolish. I sat and
Wondered. What thoughts had I when I
Watched her smile? More perplexed than
Ever, I stared as he busily worked at
The desk. But still I wondered and
Stared. I moved and asked. His response
Was honest. We each had seen her
And smiled.

ON REOPENING TREASURED LETTERS

I sit here.
My mind races down the street, turns
Right, turns sharply
To the rising tides and noiseless
Winds, speeds along, darts here,
Now there, turns and relaxes.
Then I see the full path.
My mind parks and steps down.

I relax on the floor making
Excuses, for tomorrow and yesterday.
I dared not to retrace the vital step
To that path, the path we traveled.
Time says, we stumbled along and fled
To the other path, crowded, worn,
A path of suffering, wasteful souls.

ON DIVERGENT PATHS

You need not always say what your heart
Feels. A smile rises like the sun and
Brightens the day, a kiss flies across
The lee like a bird circling the sky.
A sigh foams through the world like the
Mist on a foggy day.

A smile, a kiss and you.

This my mind remembers as it sings of
Yesterday. This my soul recaptures as it
Bathes in the happiness of yesterday. These
Consume me as I soar into tomorrow.

A smile, a kiss and you.

Yesterday I awoke into today. Today I
Dressed for tomorrow, to go closer to
That path. Today I chose that beautiful
Path of life. Today I saw the truth through
The eyes of the world.

A smile, a kiss, and you.

That path leads to you. Come with
Me and see the world.

ON LOST LOVE

Exactly what am I looking for
In a marriage, a beautiful girl
To show friends when we see
The drama or performance, someone
Irresistible, desirable,
Or-

But she is now, though
Not permitted to be possessed
By love. Eternity should say
Oneness for us.

ON MY NEXT LOVE

Suddenly I look back on our yesterdays
And realize we never planned to be one.

As I wing across the continent with
My back toward yesteryear, and greet the
New horizon, I accept having been
Loved.

The joys of your presence were
The elegant simplicity of our love.

The next blossom shall be admired,
Not picked from its vine. Her
Hypnotizing fragrance shall entice me
Until my feet turn toward the
Blazing sun.

O soul of me, rip out the anguished
Pains of my loss and be silent.
Father, Great Lord, Good
Being, grant not this love to
Suffer the cross in vain.

ON TOMORROW

I offer the golden dawn. Tomorrow
Will be more golden than yesterday,
For the brilliant shimmer of tears has
Polished tomorrow with
The light of love and happiness.

Oh glorious day,
The horizon is at its peak of light,
The sun at its apex, the moon full,
The twinkling stars, glistening,

Until parted by death.

SHRUGGING AT THE BAR

This exciting something spurs me on,
Gives me that particular energy to burn
Fuel with the highest efficiency and
Leaves no residue, throws my life
Before the cross.

Where am I going? What great secret
Must I open and throw on the wind?
What race before time must I run
At such a relenting speed?

He is sure the answer is ahead. He
Sees the entire sequence of his life
Expand in panorama before him.
He shrugs and asks what it all means
And then kisses eternity for sacrifice.

I go no matter where you lead.
You are that something all in one.

ON PLUTONIC ELEGANCE

He wanted me to write about what
Jewels I saw. Jewels
Sparkle, but your brilliance
Far surpasses the brightness of the North
Star, far outshines a polished jewel,
And will outlast time.

What can I say? Beauty is pure.
(Words tarnish plutonic elegance.)
In a small way, I venture to
Say, looking far into your eyes,
Your first beauty of life is reaching
Out to humanity, to give us renewed
Hope.

Fear not tomorrow and shine your
Beam into tomorrow for me.

STATUES IN PERSHING SQUARE

As I walked through Pershing Square,
I saw the homeless gathered there.
I saw a man with pipe in mouth
And hair tied behind his head.

They sit and read and read and sit
And eat and eat. The women knit
And pass day in and day out like this.
And feed the pigeons flying by.

They seem to have no place to go.
They seem to think but not to know
That they must act and start to live
Instead of this, being statues.

WISHES IN TIME AND SPACE

I wish that I could be with you,
Away on the hillside there
To reveal to you my thoughts of love,
As I gently caress your hair.

To tell my life's passion
My hopes for our success.
If the wind would blow across your face,
Our love it would bless.

I remember we were apart,
Our lips would never meet
But now our lips are close in love
Beneath the cold winter heat.

May it permit this bliss
To last year to year,
As we walk through life as one,
Each moment is extremely dear.

ON REGAINED LIFE

I cannot live without my unique
Love, yet, she decided not to
Make the journey with me. How can
I readjust my life to thoughts,
Memories, despair, hopes, fears,
Realities and tomorrows?

I think somehow my loss shall be
My greatest reward when I reach
Over and accept.

AFTER THE FIRST KISS

Come dance with me my first loved one,
Come dance with me today.
To follow you over the hill,
To sing and dance and play.

I feel as though we own the world, as
My heart leaps to and fro.
My feet touch down upon the ground,
With a love that's joy to know.

REACHING BEYOND ETERNITY

I need to endure, to persevere in life
And grab for rocks of strength,
To stay with none but me around,
To remember, dance, to sing.

This week I will cut that bond of life
And run to dark decay.
To see all the failures
Disguised as yesterday.

GREATER THAN THE SUM

A dangerous man may be that
Man to accomplish the task and set
The next mission for tomorrow.

But brave men do their deeds
Their way and forget the wisdom
They were taught in the past.

Yet desperate and brave at once,
We may have one act to
Live and live to act again.

ON RESPECT

Rewards or great credits are
Not deserved, just respect.
Respect, more than a polite doing as had
Been done before, or more than one
Did. Respect is pride,
In accomplishing the task.
Respect is Gratitude.

ON CONCERN

Be I cynic or not, my first
Concern is for the other,
Be they here or far away. My mind
Reaches as far as my heart can
Beat, but my smallness
Can never reach far enough to
Include all. My sadness
Follows through life.

ON APPEARANCE OF SADNESS

Whenever tears come to my eyes,
I smile. In an appearance
Of sadness, I remember the happiest
Second, that moment with you.
I cherish that one moment more
Than I cherish any other. It was
Then I realized our love, an ever
Lasting relationship in life.

ON FINDING A CLUE

I wonder as to the why of me. If I ask
Others, they'l tell me why they
Like or hate me, But some-
Where, there is an answer to the core
Of the why of me. I search and find no
Answer, no clue to me.

ON DELIVERANCE OF CHILDREN

At this hour, oneness is assured.

At this hour, oneness is assured.
I hear the singing of truth
Amid the ruins of past
Mistakes, wars and conquests.

At this hour, the wandering
Youths fight for tomorrow and
Look at the destroyers of today
As they shape our paths of deliverance.

Deceit and knowledge are bred in
A flashlight and gun, searching for
The threat of the light of nights as it
Crawls toward the oneness of the nuns.

Deliverance is ours if only one escapes,
If only one baby cries a final scream and
Stands taller tomorrow, if only a novice
Escape with the child of hope.

A secluded haven is known to the world.
Here, a song travels to Him on high.
A decent night's sleep comes to the child.
Tomorrow may bring treason and the enemy.

Out of the haven into heaven
With the assurance of the Blessed
Mother, the Master has come to
Bathe the Earth with blood of the child.

The new commandant has come to
Protect the garrison and continue the
Death of millions of children, those,
The Master wishes to cleanse with death.

A mission to overwhelm the body
While the mind wills to continue.
Then, we shall see victory and taste of
Tomorrow. Success is ours, assuredly.

Blessed Mother, Holy Mary, and the
Nun shall perform the duties
Of the saint and leave the rosary
For the children of deliverance.

FROM A SAILOR SON

Under the Christmas tree, may it seem bare,
No present from your son wrapped there.
Uncle Sam has taken me away,
And into my pockets puts so little pay.

From coast to coast rings out the tune
I sent at thanksgiving. It's not too soon
To say I miss you at Christmas time,
To sing songs, say the prayer and dine.

Every star that shines with heavenly light
Sparkles with my message on this night.
All the presents and gifts I haven't sent,
All the tidings and wishes they represent,
Say Merry Christmas and Happy New Year
From a sailor son, to Dad and Mother Dear.

NAVY LIFE AFTER TAPS

Where I wonder, do those ladders lead?
Is anyone standing topside?
Why are the passageways dark?
It's Navy life after taps.

From where does all the quiet come?
Does he sit at the desk all alone?
No lights, no noise, no commotion,
It's Navy life after taps.

They are sacking out and sleeping,
They are watching, searching and identifying
The creatures who roam after dark.

They are challenging and saluting.
They are testing, teaching and training
Against the enemies of the nation.

They are the Navy team of life,
Assuring our Nation's safety,
Our return to Colors,
They are Security, Safety, and Men.

HIGHWAY ONE-OH-ONE

Out of here, away from the military
Guardians of me, out to the underpass,
Out to the Pacific Ocean.

Noon time, out to the south and
The white ruffled petticoat on to sun
Scorched sands of winter, then up and
Under the overpass, on highway one-oh-one.

Pines, shrubs, waves and brush, false
Greens of winter, blue lake and
Home for mud hens and mud friends, A
View of sky meeting the ocean.

A white-blue gleam of the ocean reflecting
The green-white gleam of the sky.

The whirling sand and ocean, Encinitas,
-Nitas, -nitas. The flat sand with
Strollers, walkers and pushers of
Strollers, and mothers.

The Pacific, South Pacific, Bali Hai,
Hai Lai, mountains out to the sky,
Pago Pago and eighteen more, Bahia and

Marine Bay lead down to the shore. The
Splashing surf slashes its tail
In the sand pushing a mighty spray onto the bluffs
At Torrey Pines.
The split mountain for the in between
Pass to the overpass and the pulse of
Nature, the Queen.

Putting putters and flying flyers aim
For the blue. General Dynamics and the
Rotunda of Structure (blue in a core
Of power) lead to La Jolla and La Pacifica.

Across a ravine, and conformity,
Villa Marina, sleek serenity.

Bypass the overpass and ride the
Signs of living away from the ocean,
The straight away from marine life,
Balboa Park and animal motion.

The masts of ships deck the bay
Before you turn onto Broadway.

A WATCH ON LIFE AND DEATH

I was not born to die for fame,
But to live, revere my name,
To do the job, perform the deeds,
To earn my wage, supply my needs.

To raise a family with lots of care,
To sire a captain, if we should dare,
To laugh by day, cry by night,
Protect the earnings win the fight.

To go to church, escape the hell,
Eat the dinner, smoke and tell,
To wash the car, mow the lawn,
Share the kiss before the dawn.

To raise my children, a princess or two,
Raise them saintly, as a mother would do,
To go to heaven, present my card,
Leave the family under the care of G O D.

To meet the saints, enter the gate,
Enjoy the kingdom, as is my fate,
To see the names upon the scroll,
Smile with friends as the bell tolls.

To look below and see the day,
When all ascend this way,
To greet them all, caress my wife,
Continue the reign for all my life.

ACKNOWLEDGEMENT

Realization Of Us
   Published March 1960 Vol. IV, No. 1, Bardic Echoes
The Art Of Painting
   Published in Scimitar and Song, No Carolina
Wild Wind
   Published Spring Issue of The Muse, Poetry Quarterly
Upon A Star
   Published Lyrics of Love, Best New Lovepoems 1963
Shrugging At The Bar
   Published in Scimitar and Song
Wishes In Time And Space
   Published in The Anthology Of American Poetry

www.ingramcontent.com/pod-product-compliance
Lightning Source LLC
Chambersburg PA
CBHW060719030426
42337CB00017B/2924